I0473032

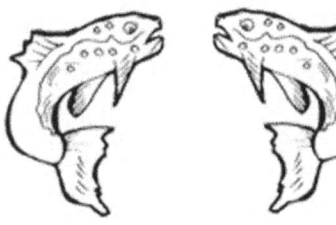

This is an illustrated work of fiction. Characters, businesses, places, events, locales, and incidents are used in a fictitious manner. Any resemblance to actual persons, living or dead, or actual events, could be purely coincidental with the exception of those who agreed to have their likeness depicted for the sake of art. However, the illustrations were inspired by places, events & People of Humboldt County.

Copyright© 2018 K.M. Myers
Copyright© 2022 K.M. Myers
All rights reserved.

Published in the United States by K.M. Publishing, Humboldt County, California.

ISBN-13: 978-0692069325
ISBN-10: 0692069321

Printed in the United States of America

Book Design by K.M. Myers
Production by CreateSpace

10 9 8 7 6 5 4 3 2 1
SECOND EDITION

Bigfoot in HUMBOLDT

THE ADULT COLORING BOOK
for BIGFOOT-LOVERS

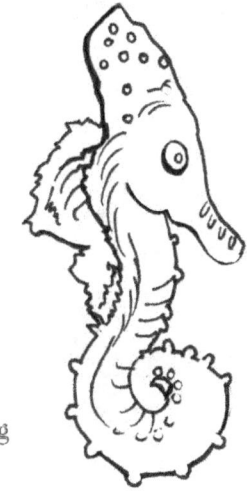

K&M Publishing
California
2018

Illustrated by K.M. Myers

Table of Contents

"Bigfoot was interviewed on The Patty Winters Show this morning and to my shock I found him surprisingly articulate and charming."
Bret Easton Ellis, American Psycho

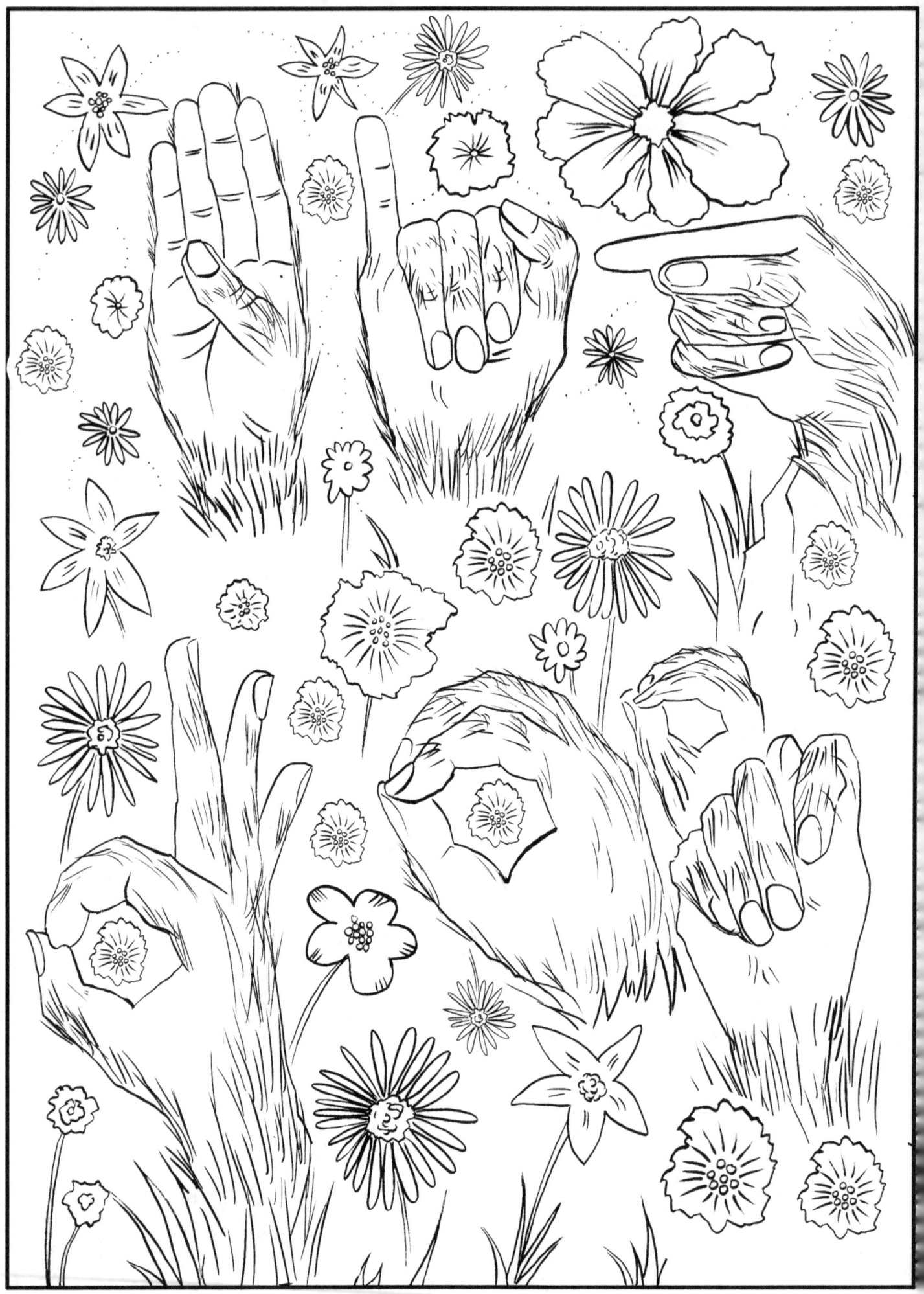

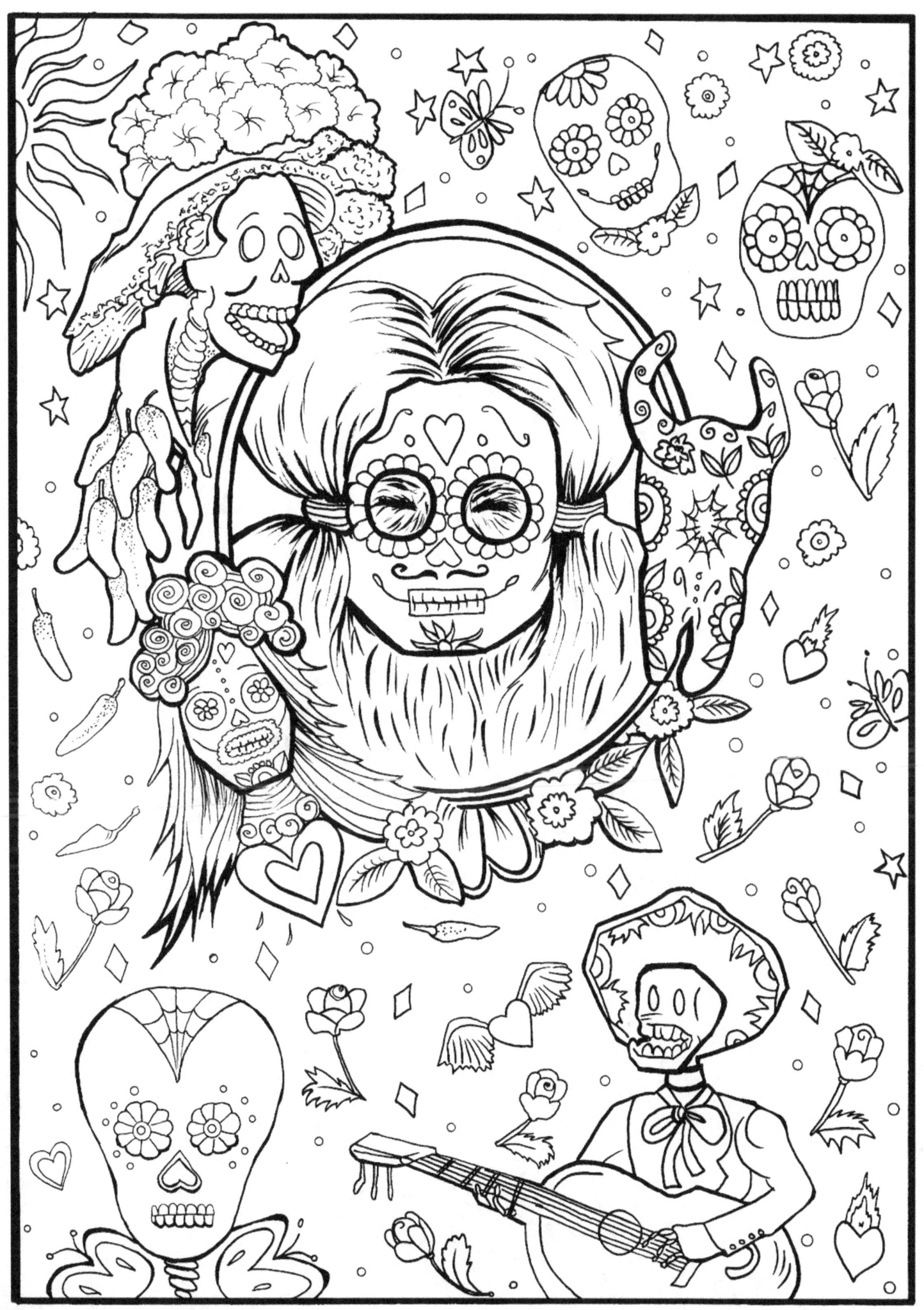

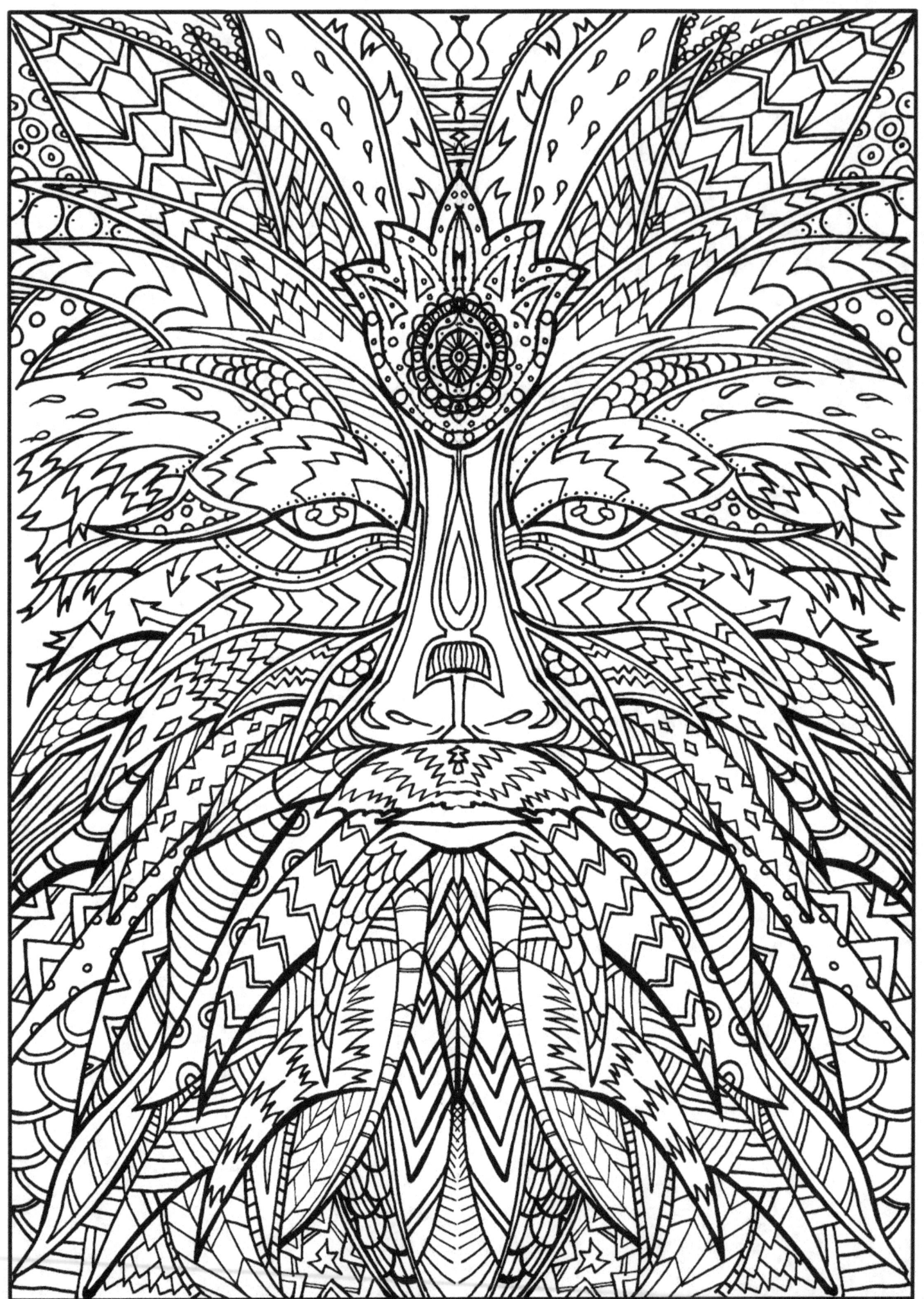

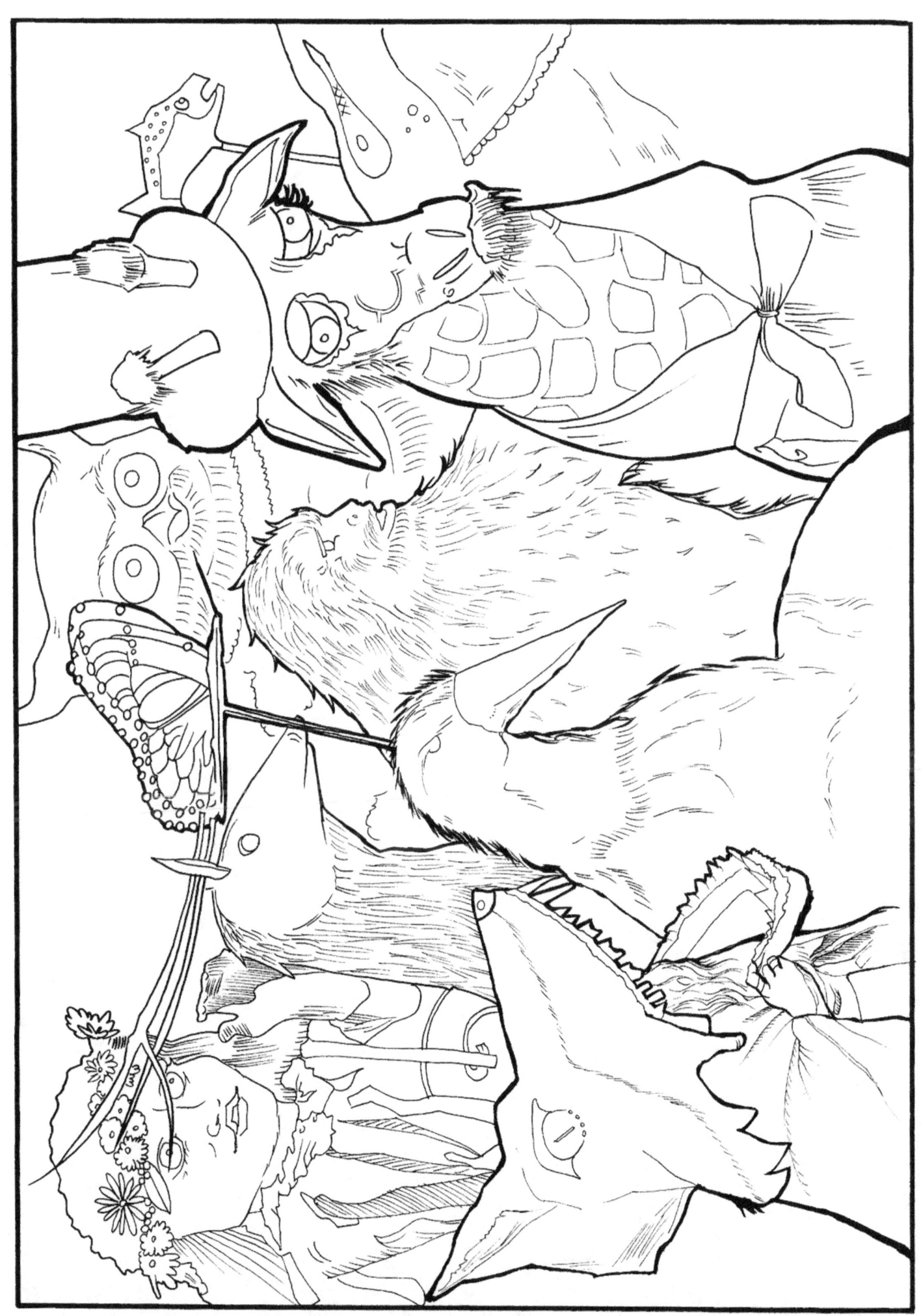

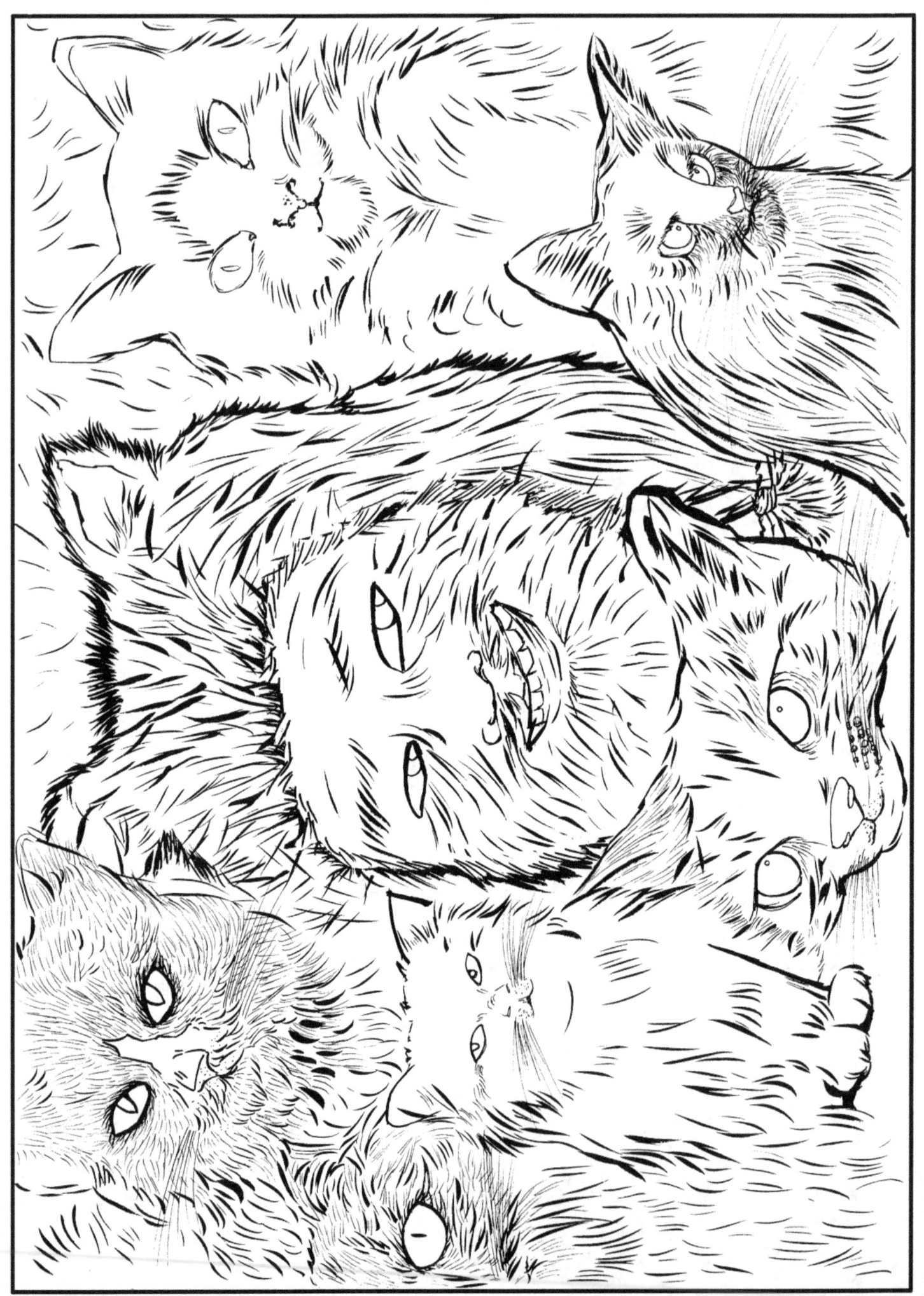

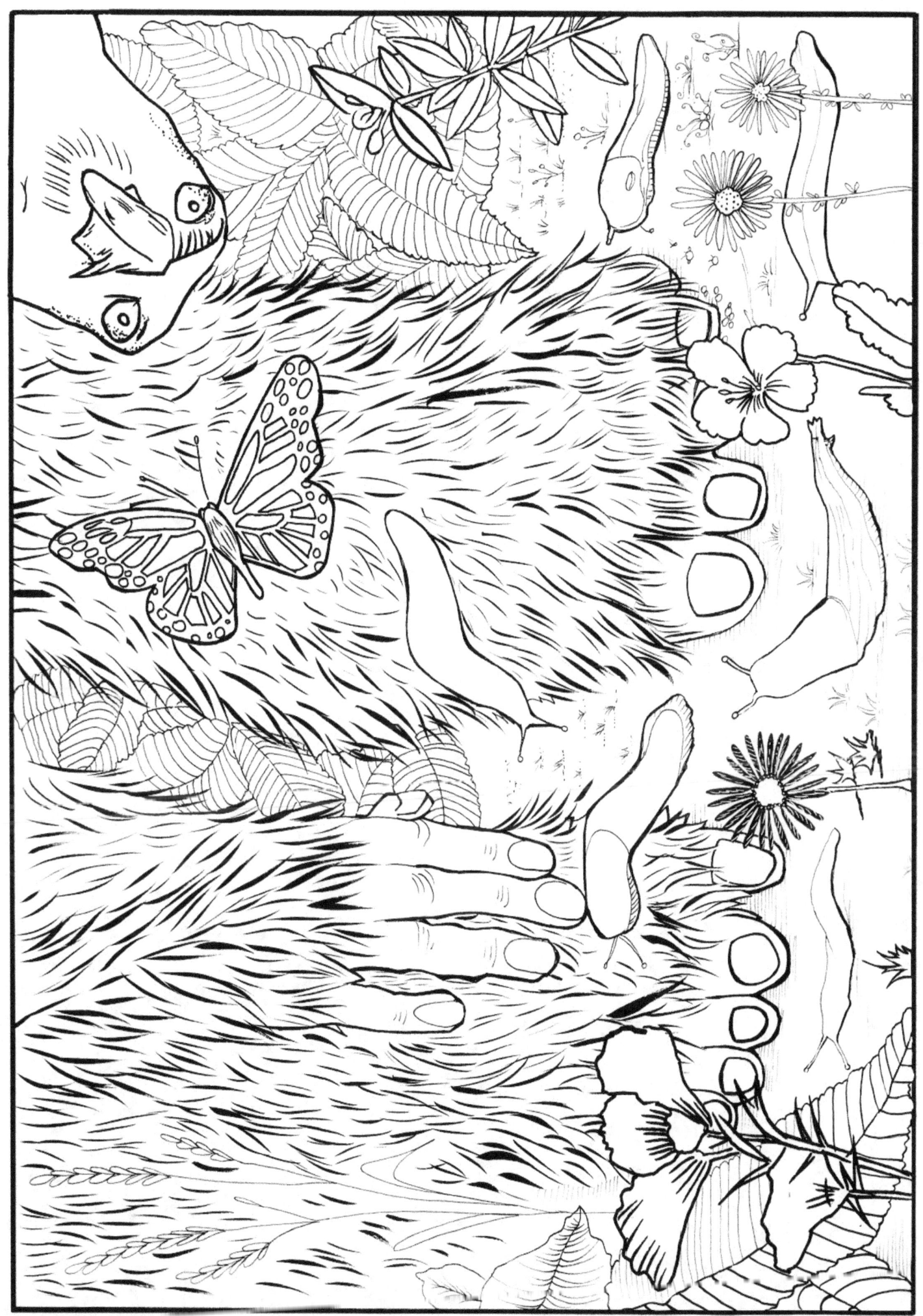

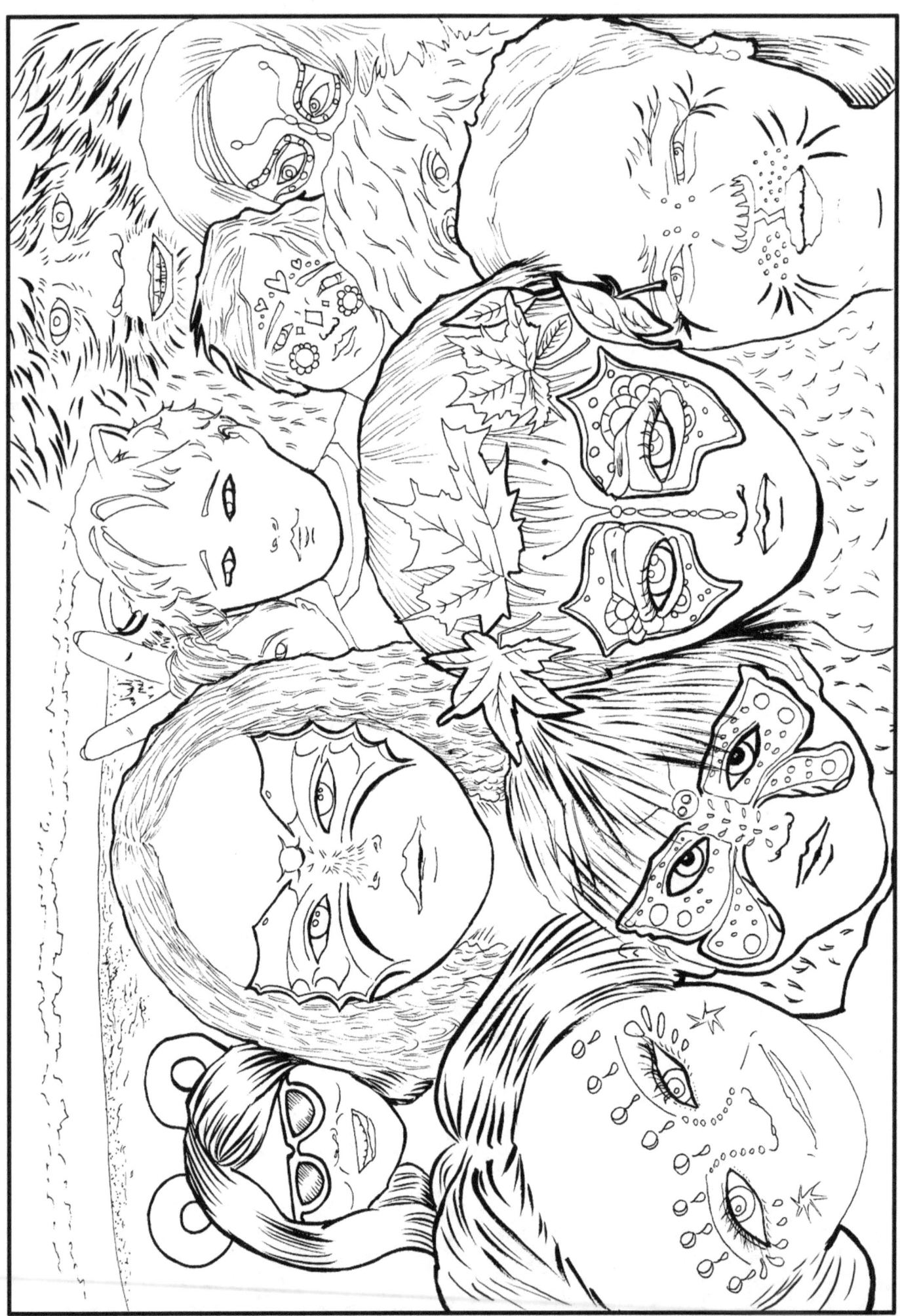

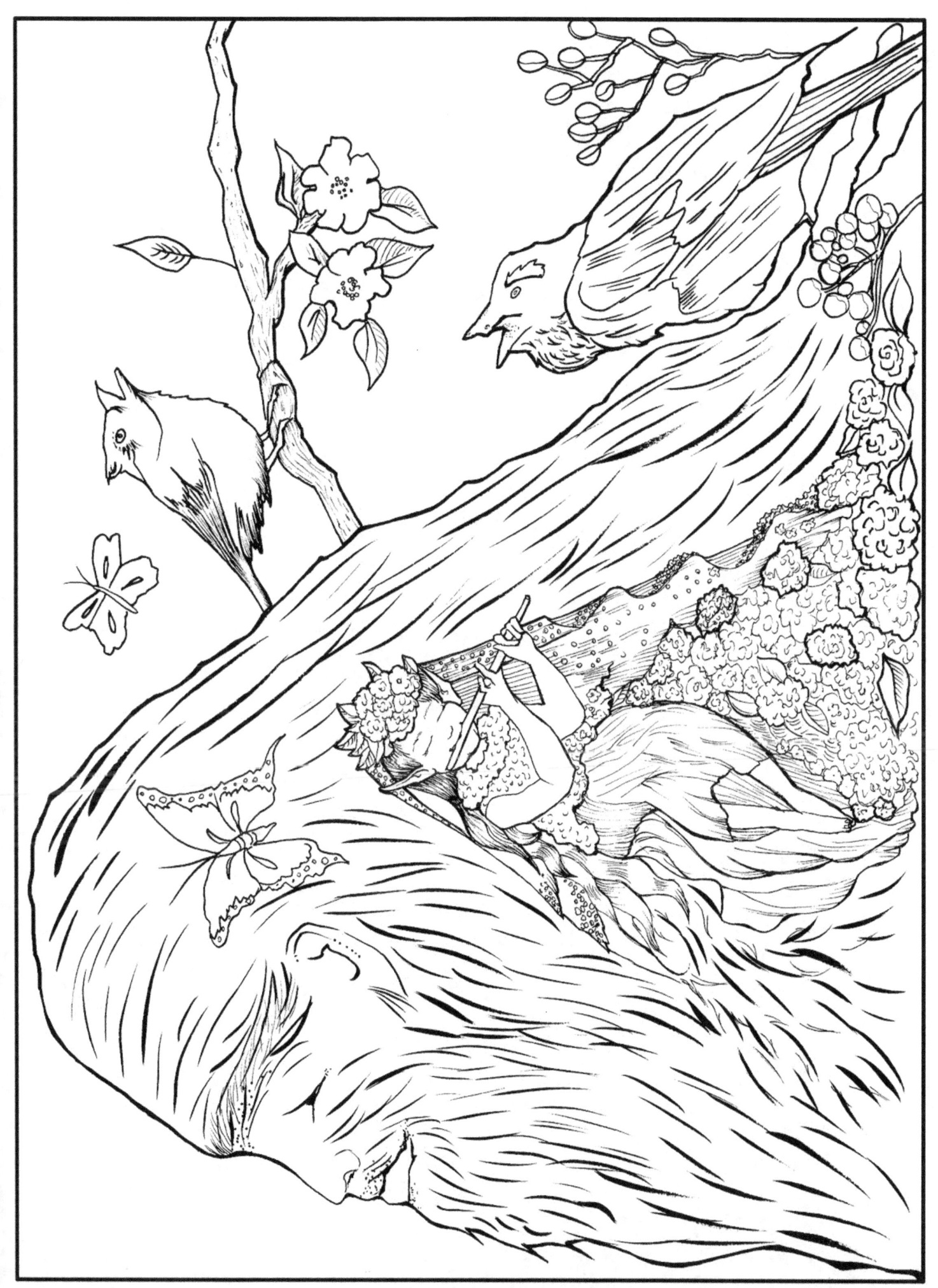

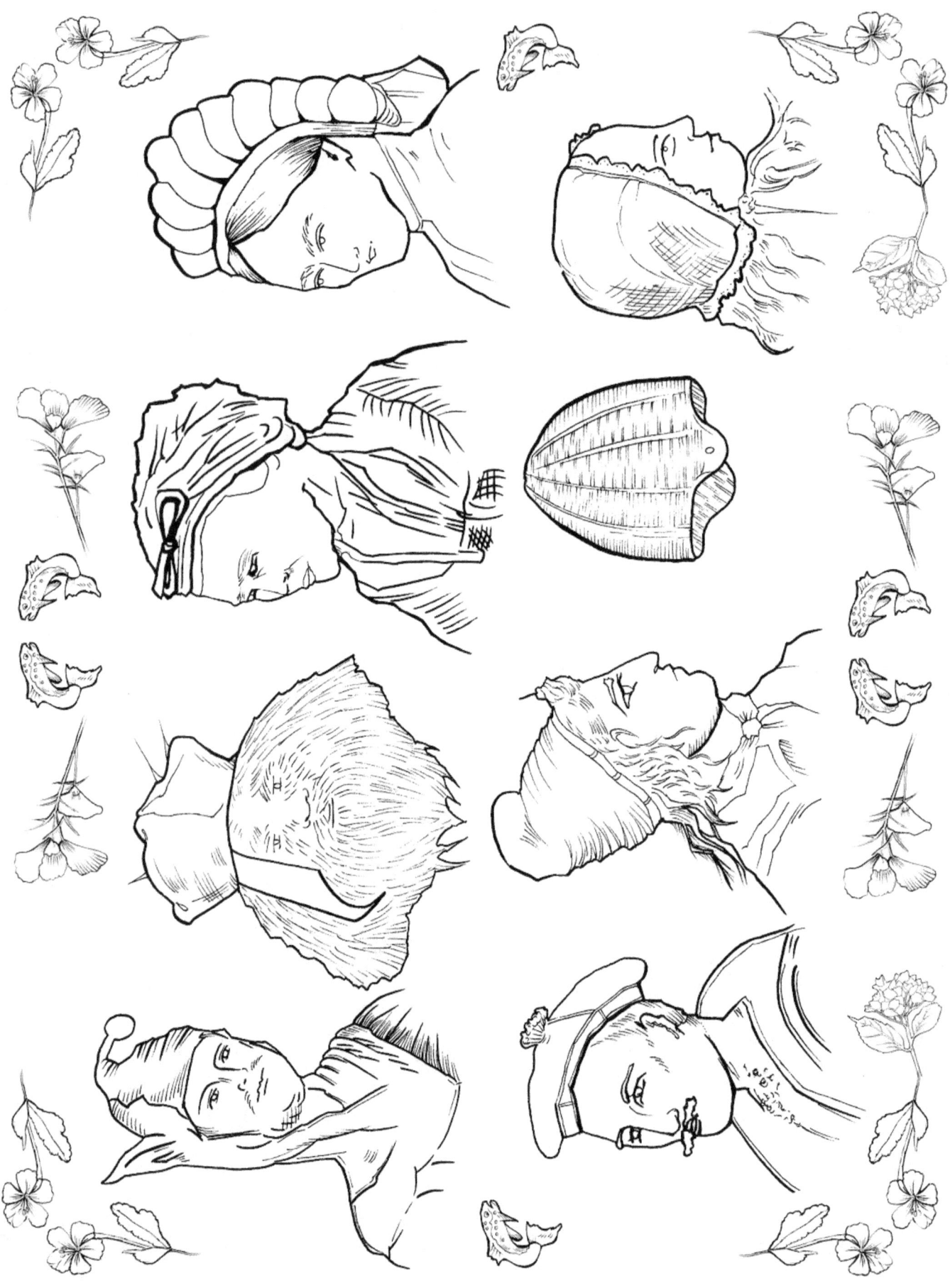

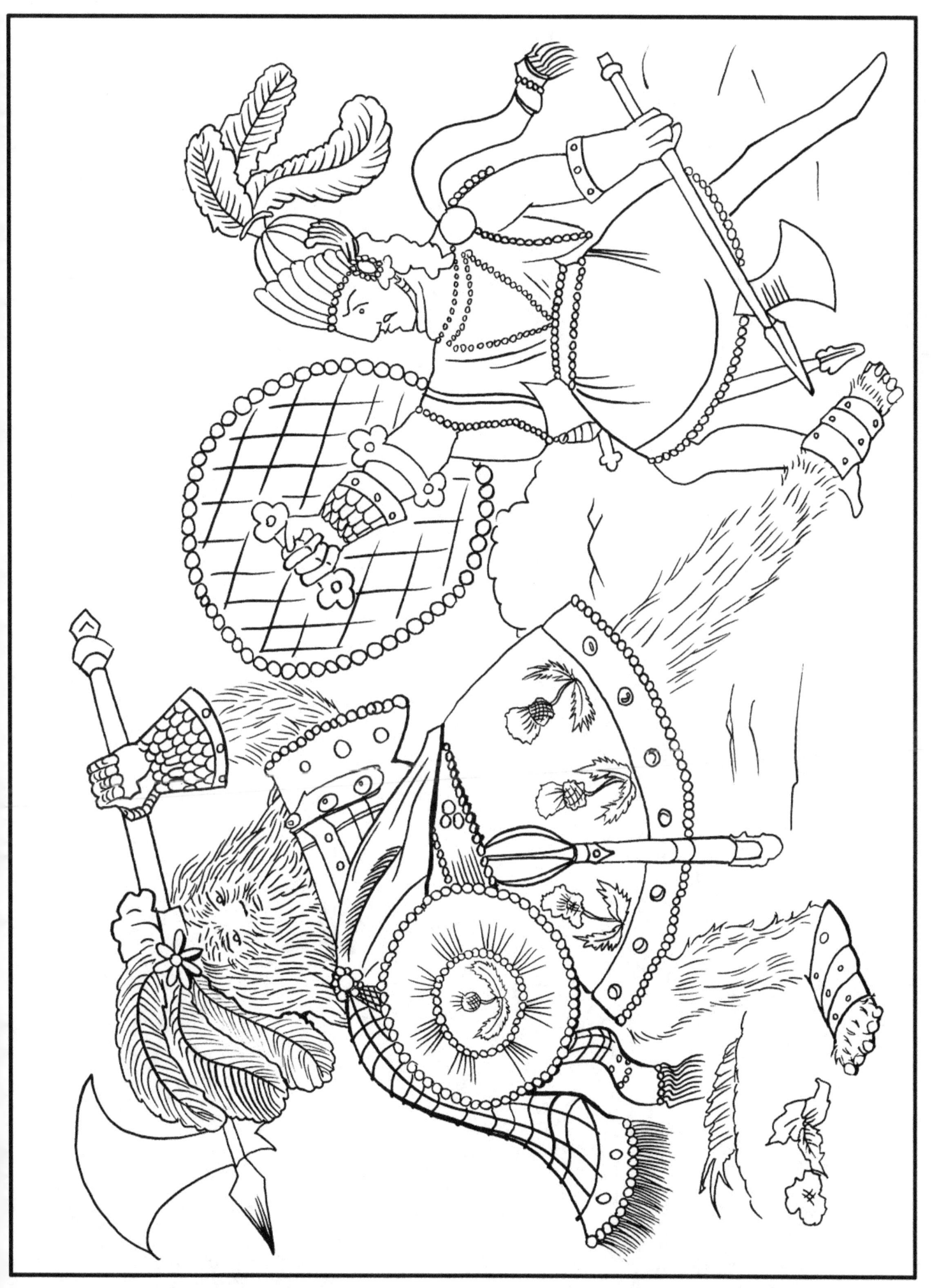

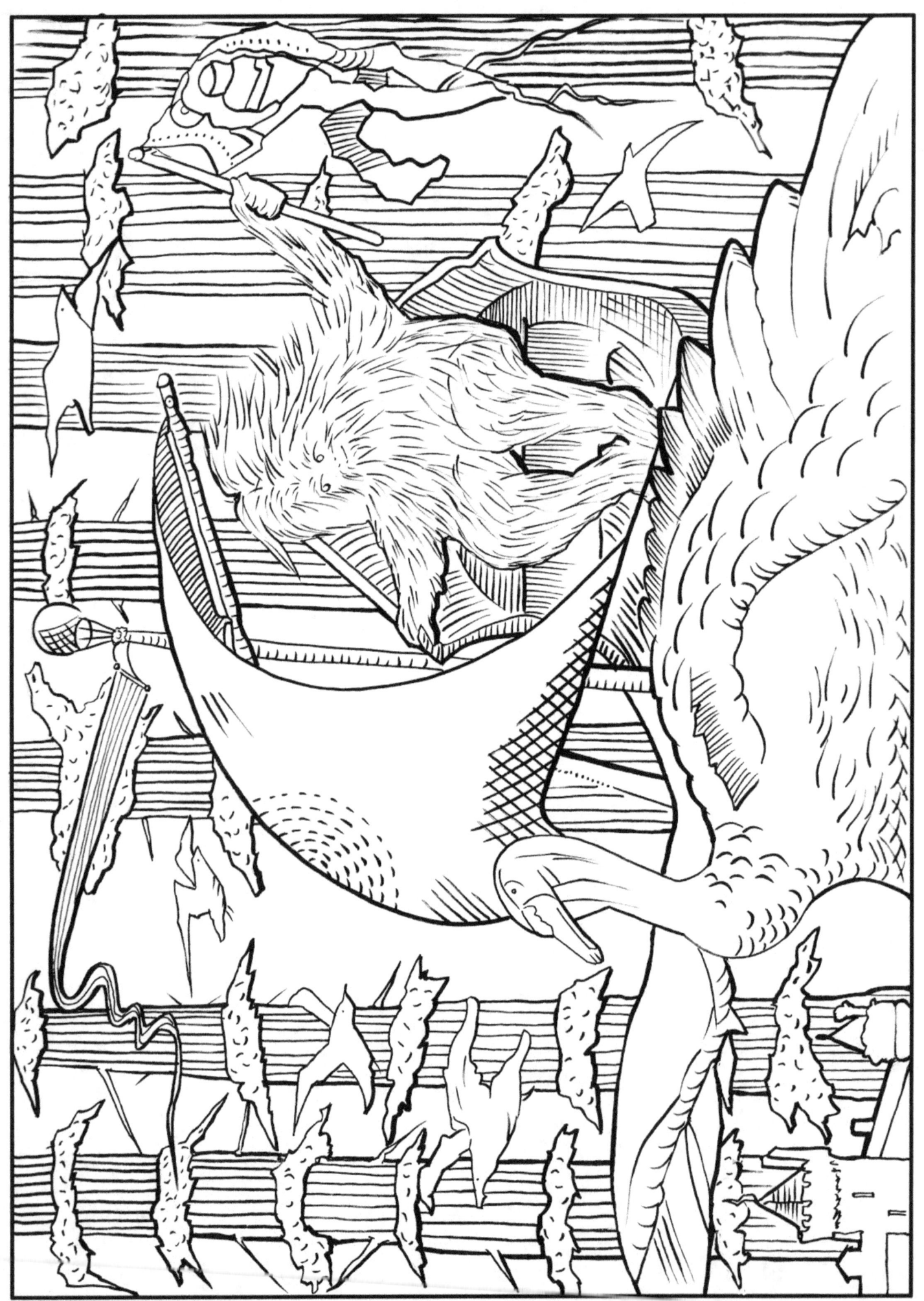

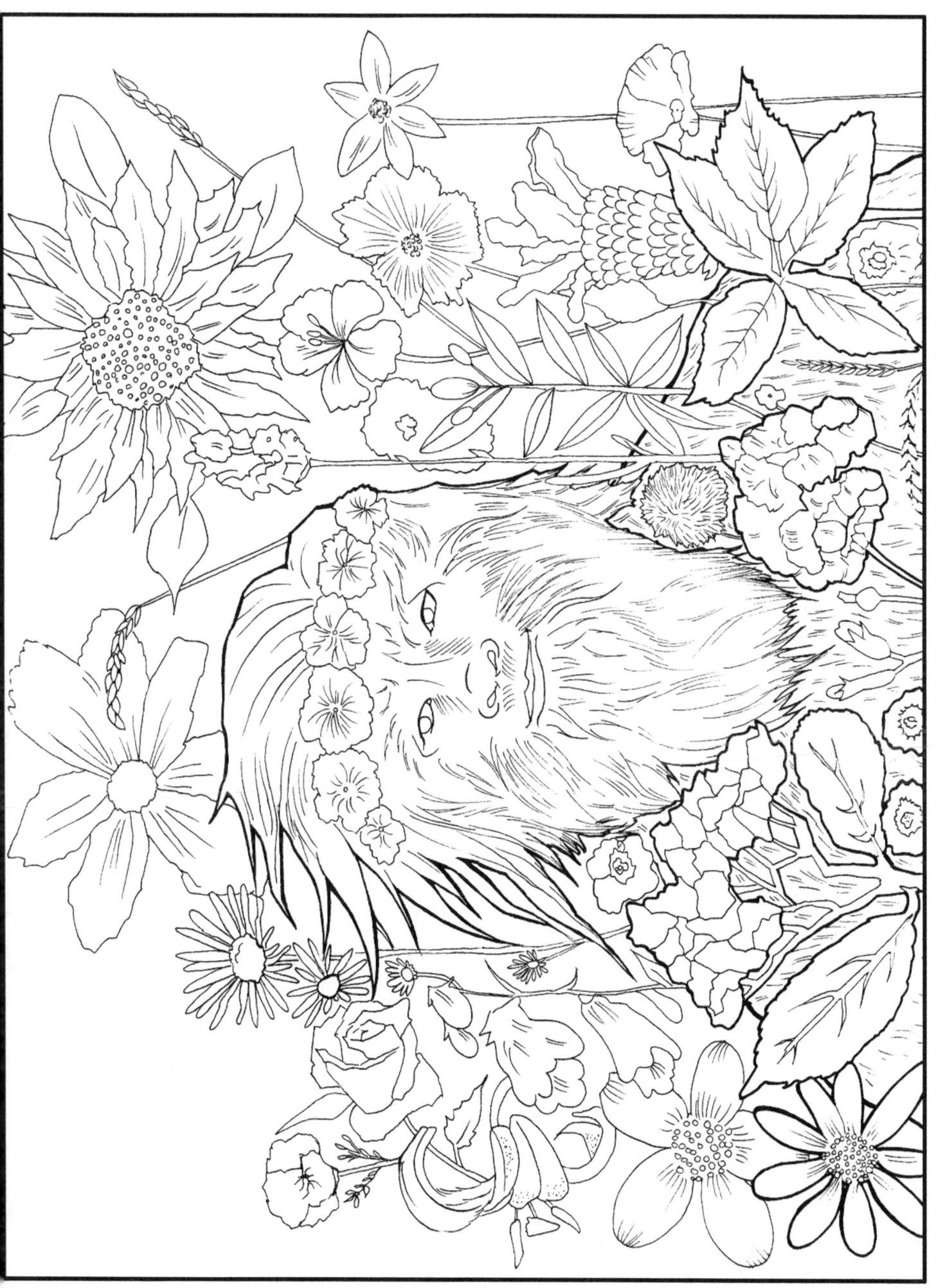

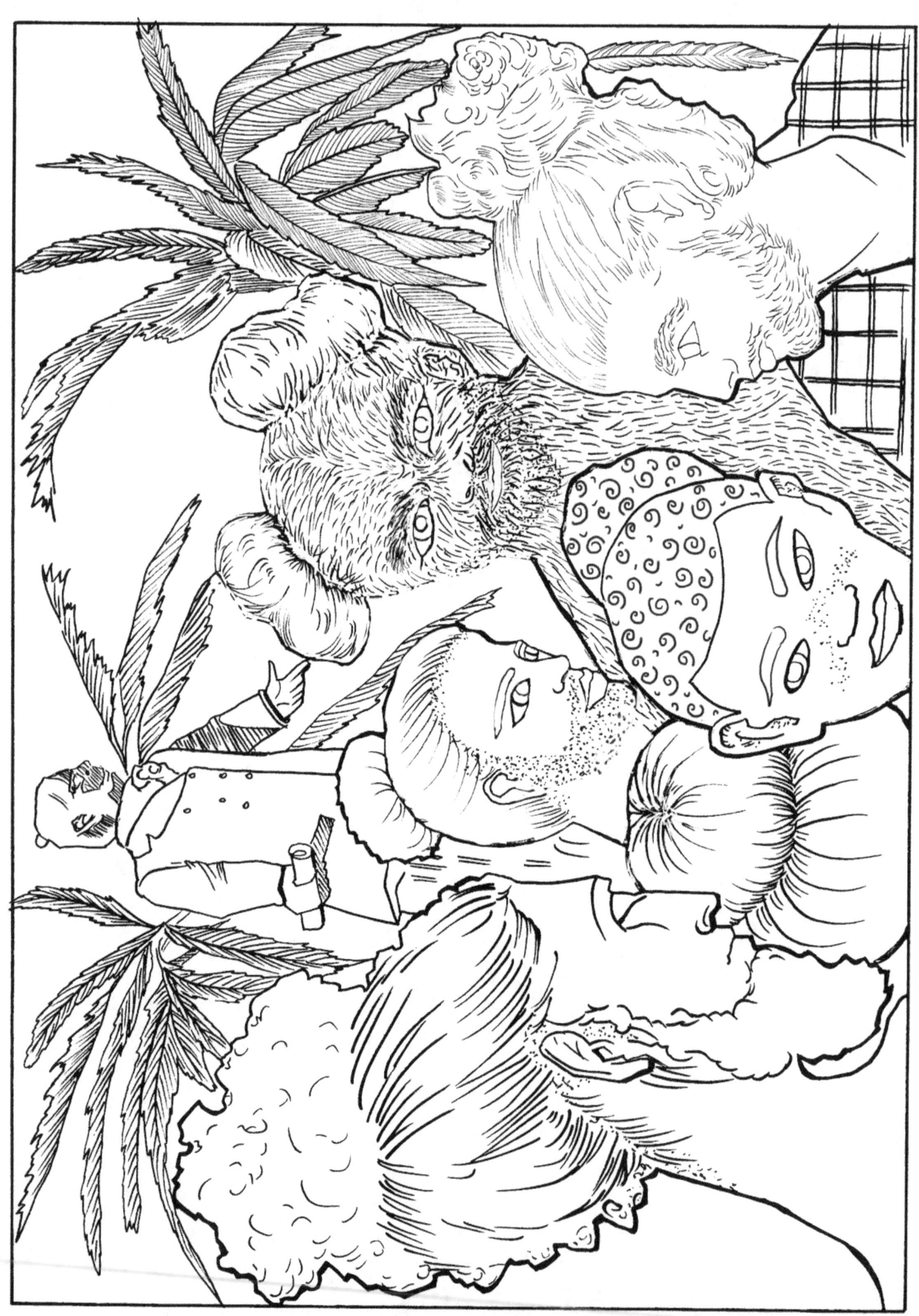

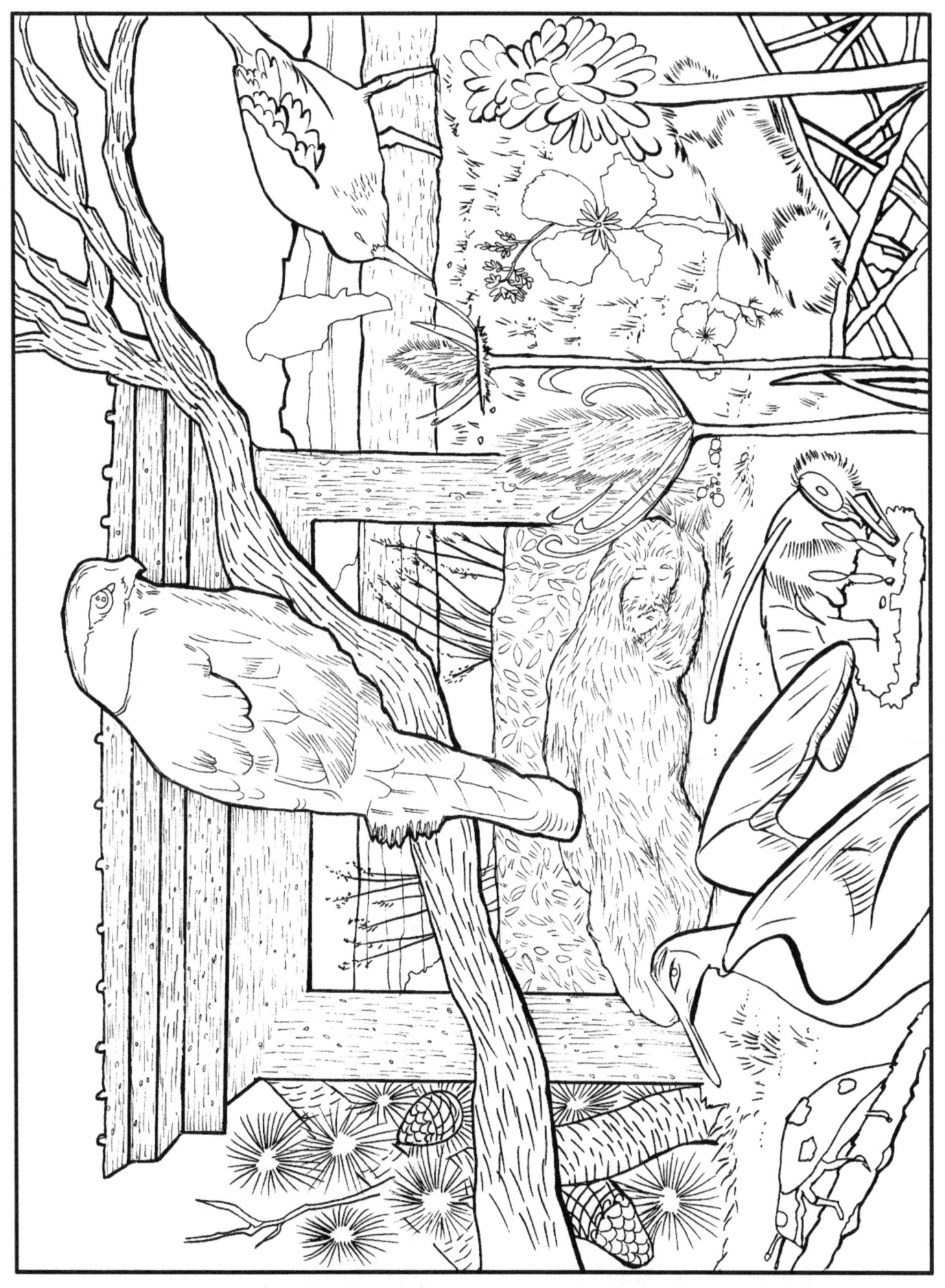

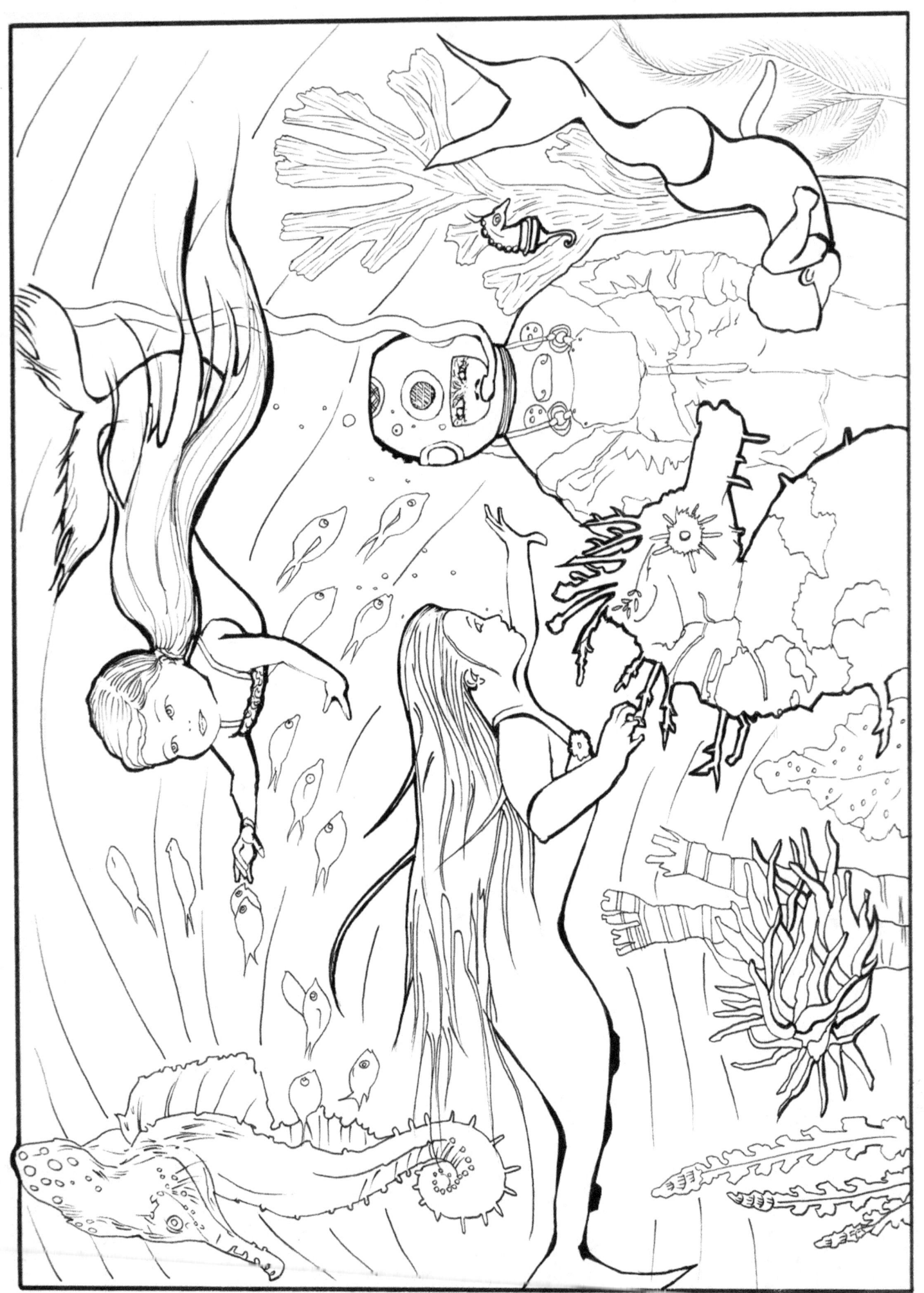

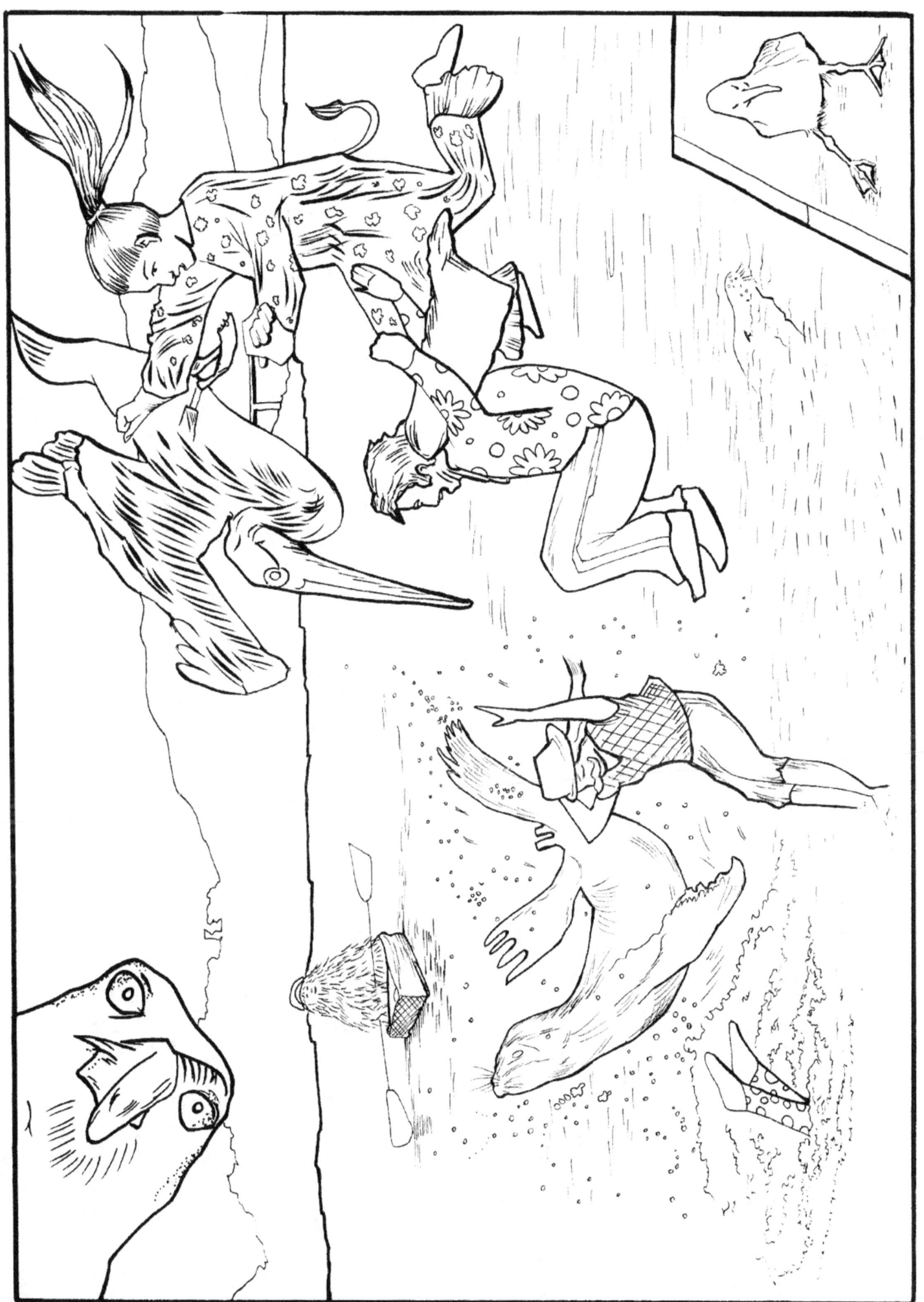

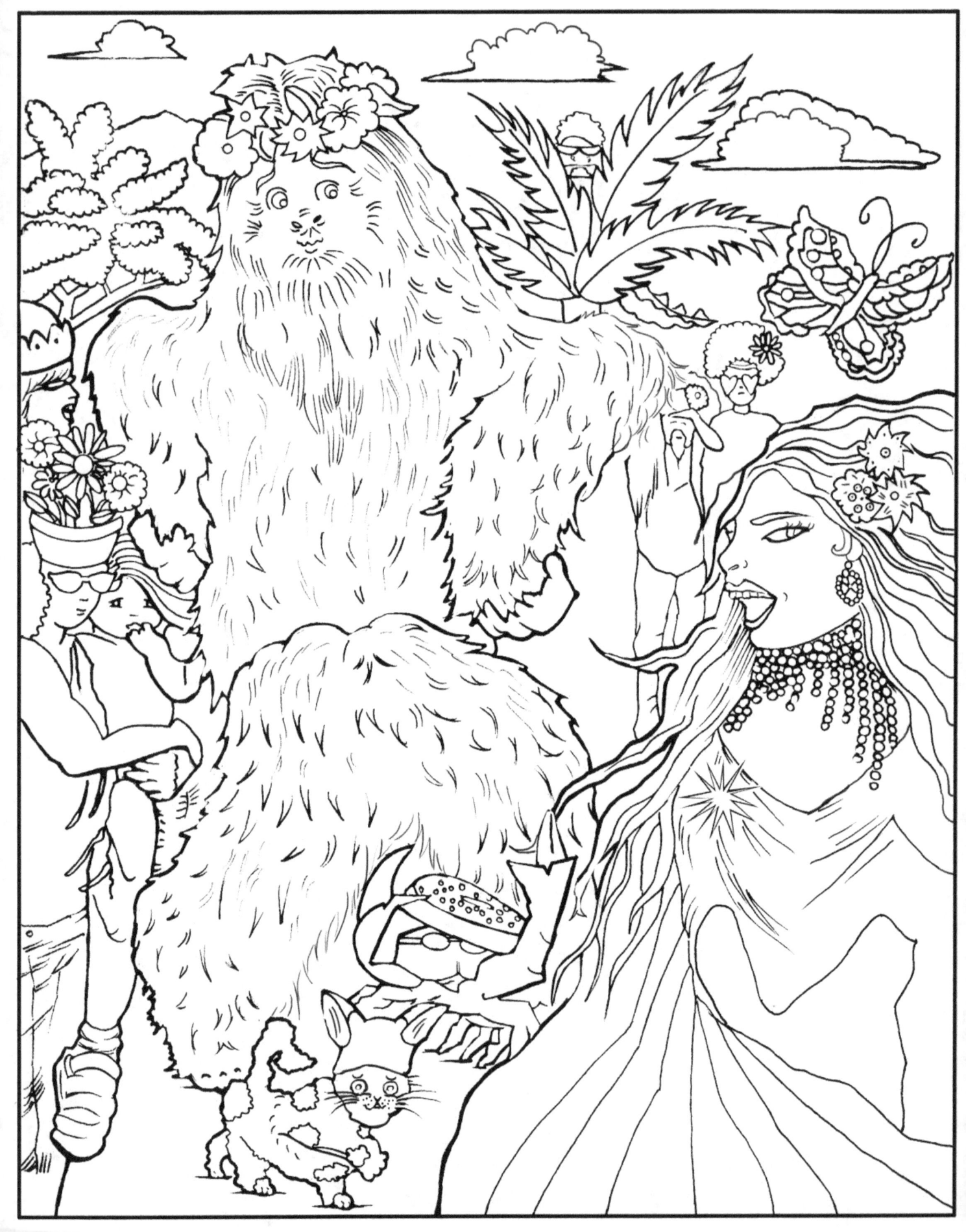

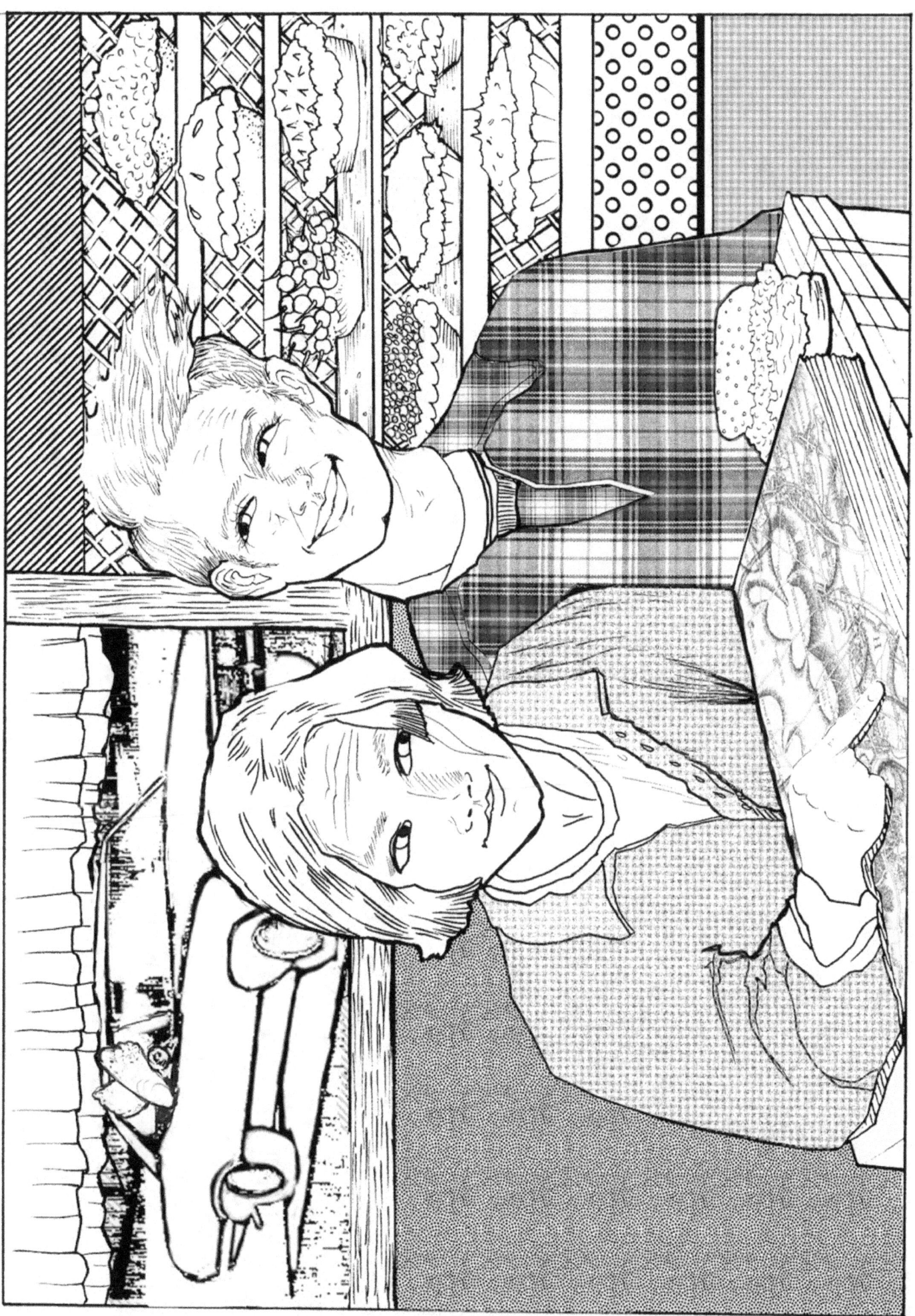

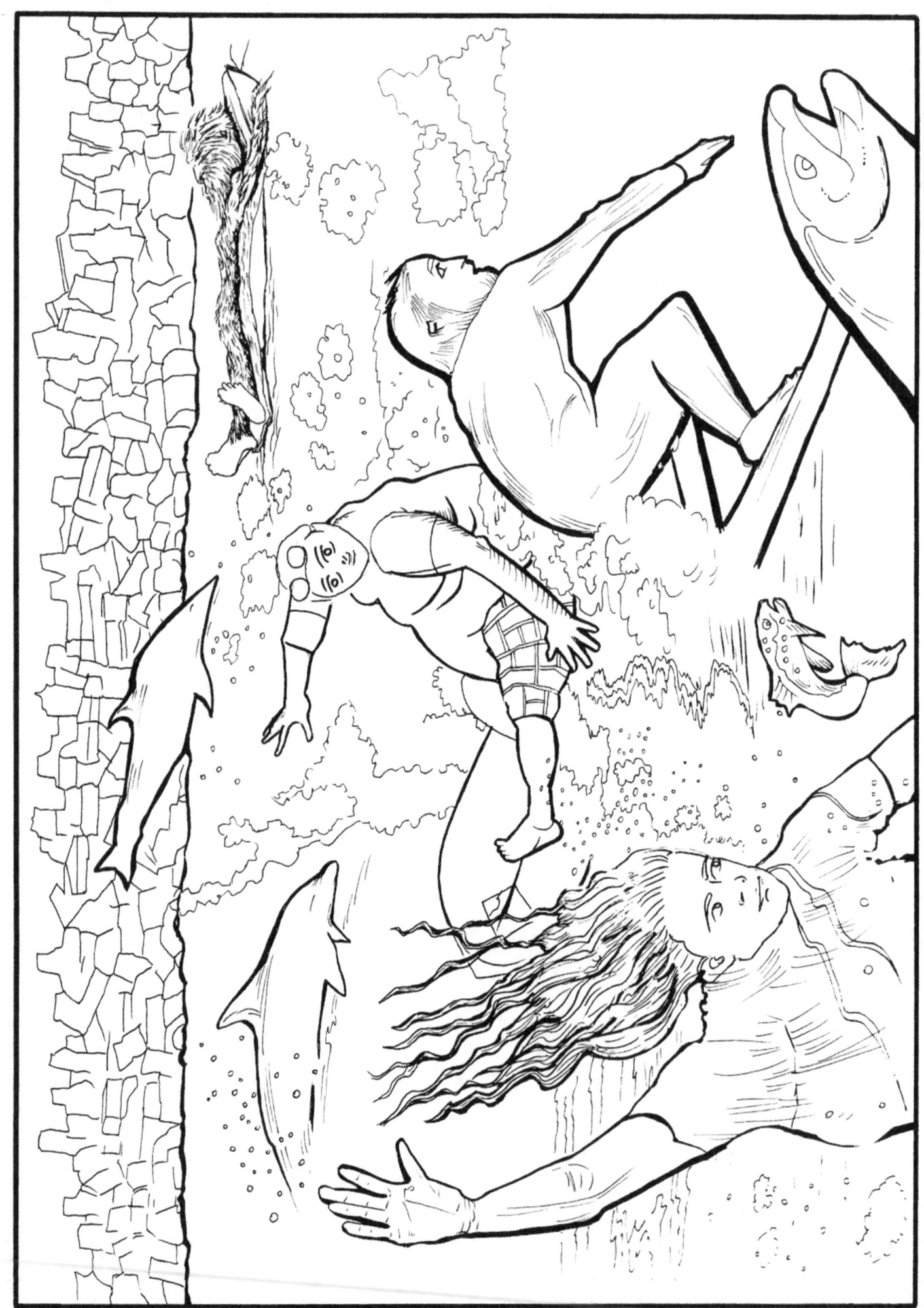

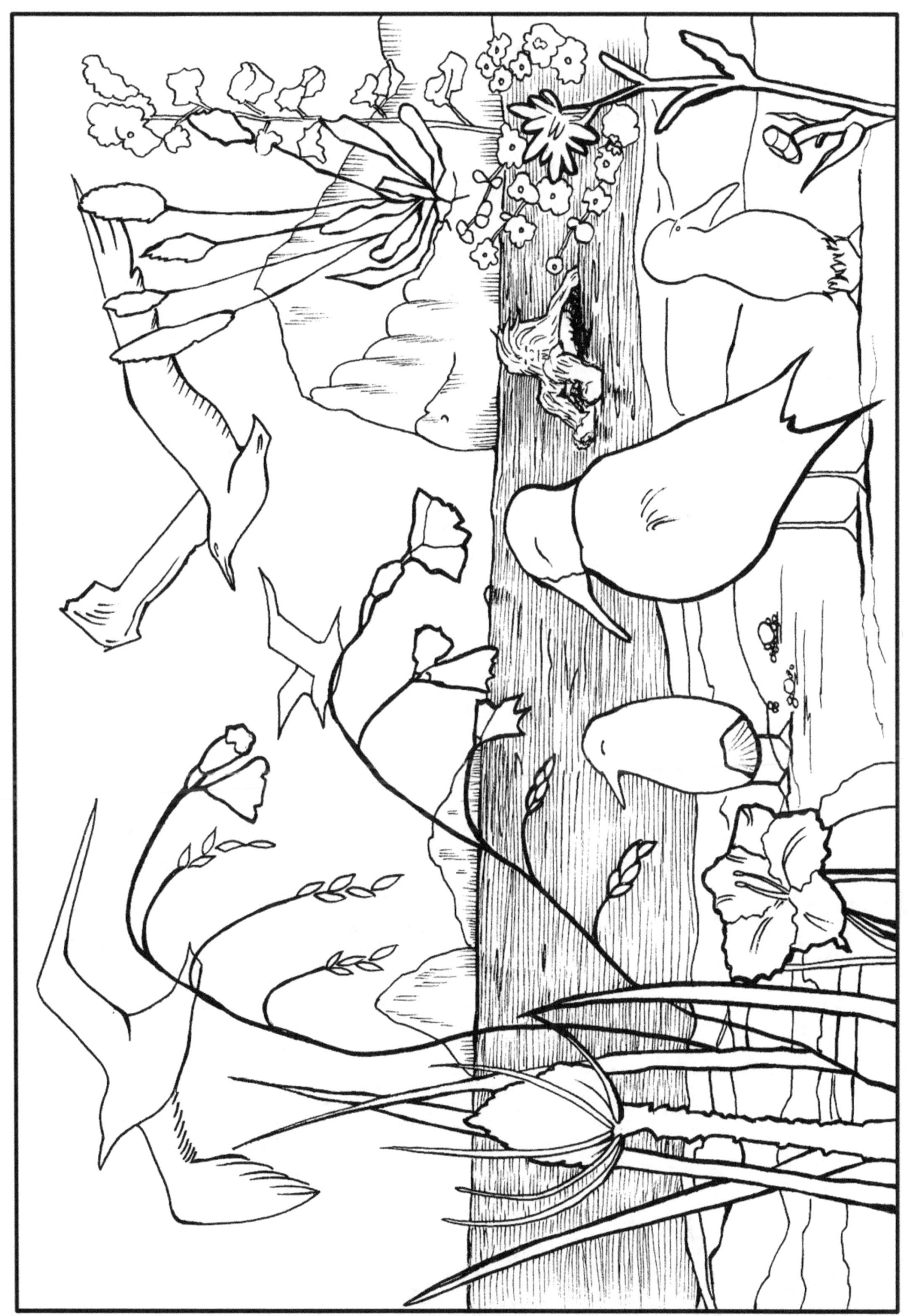

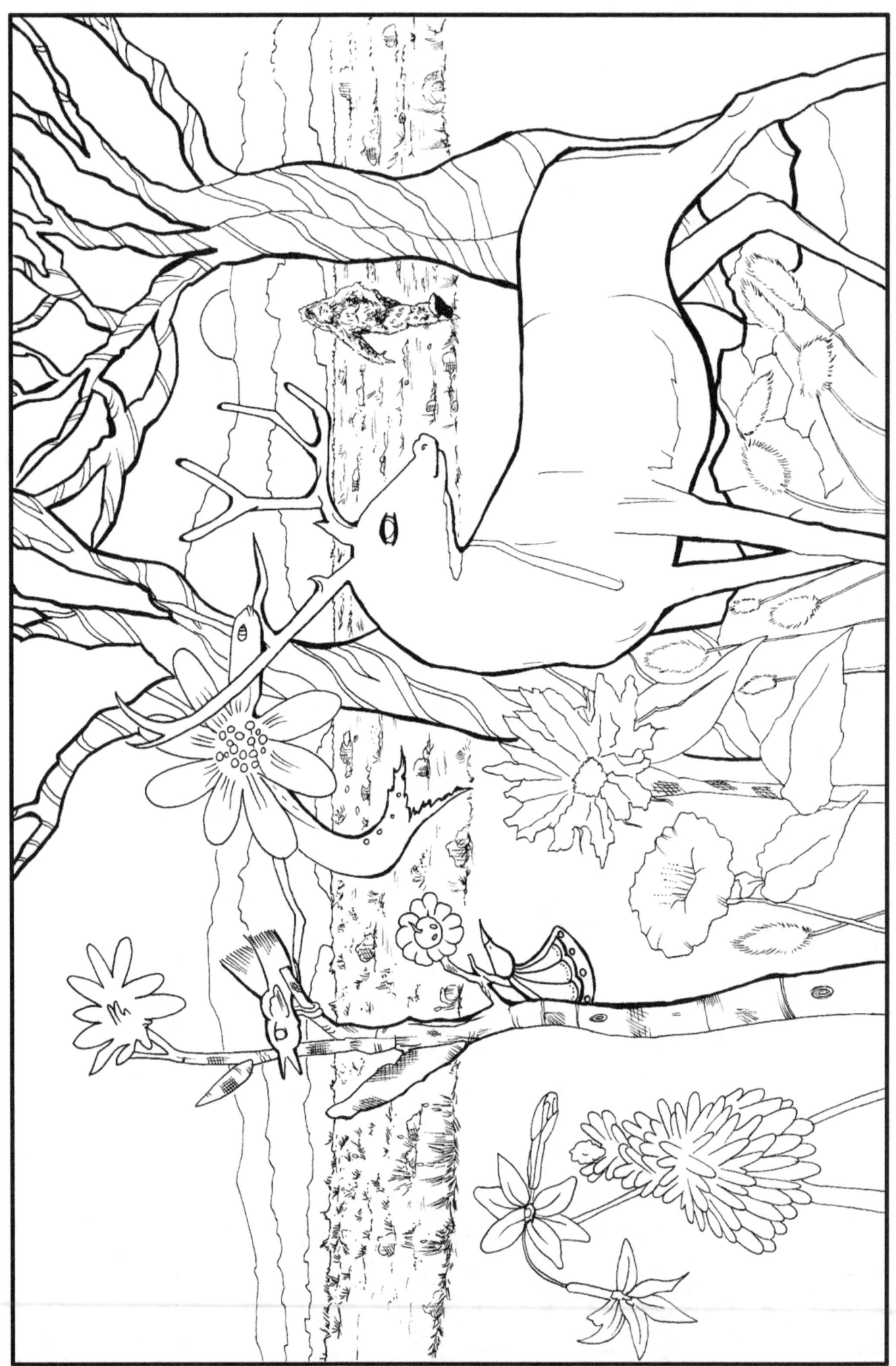

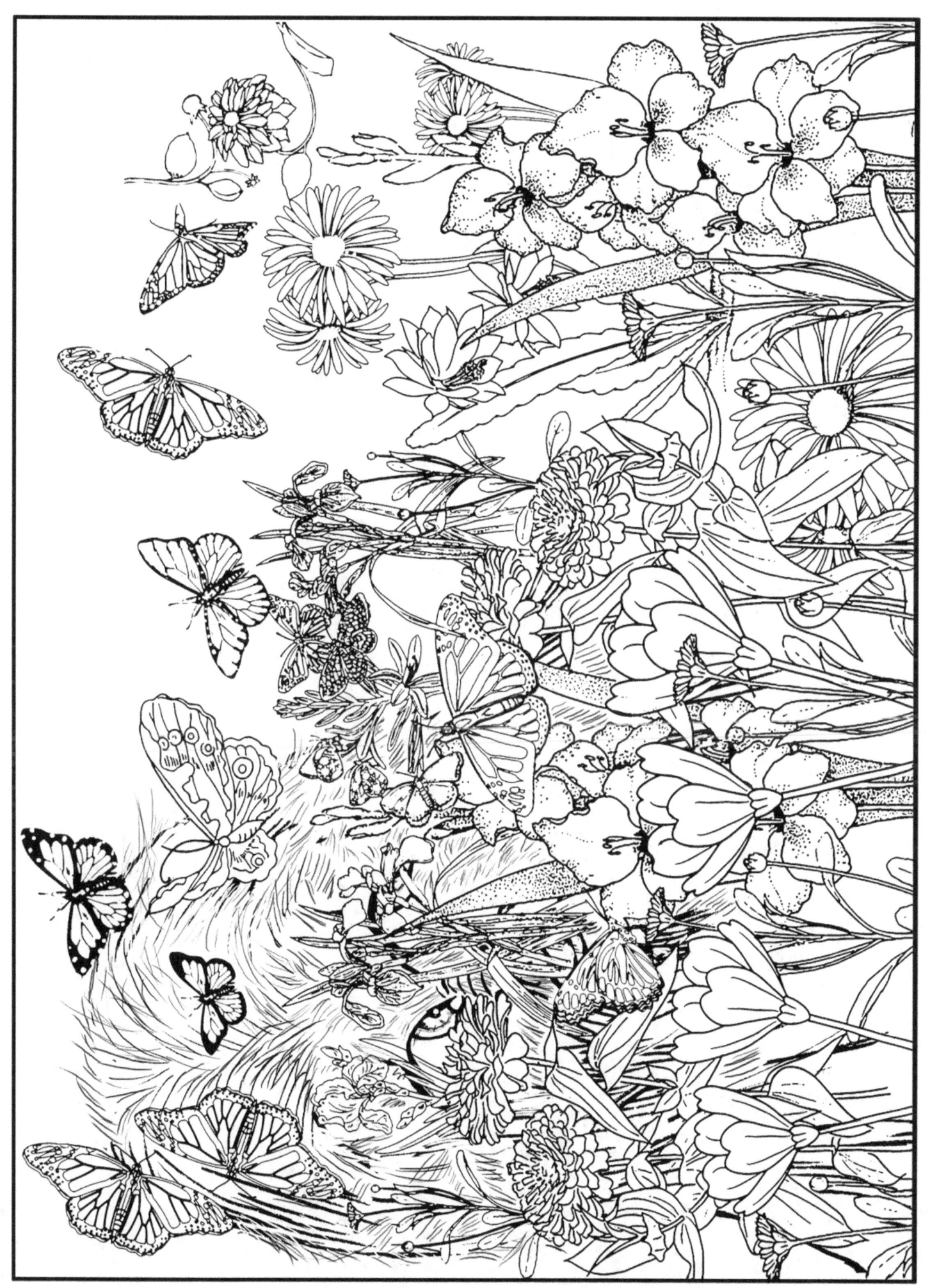

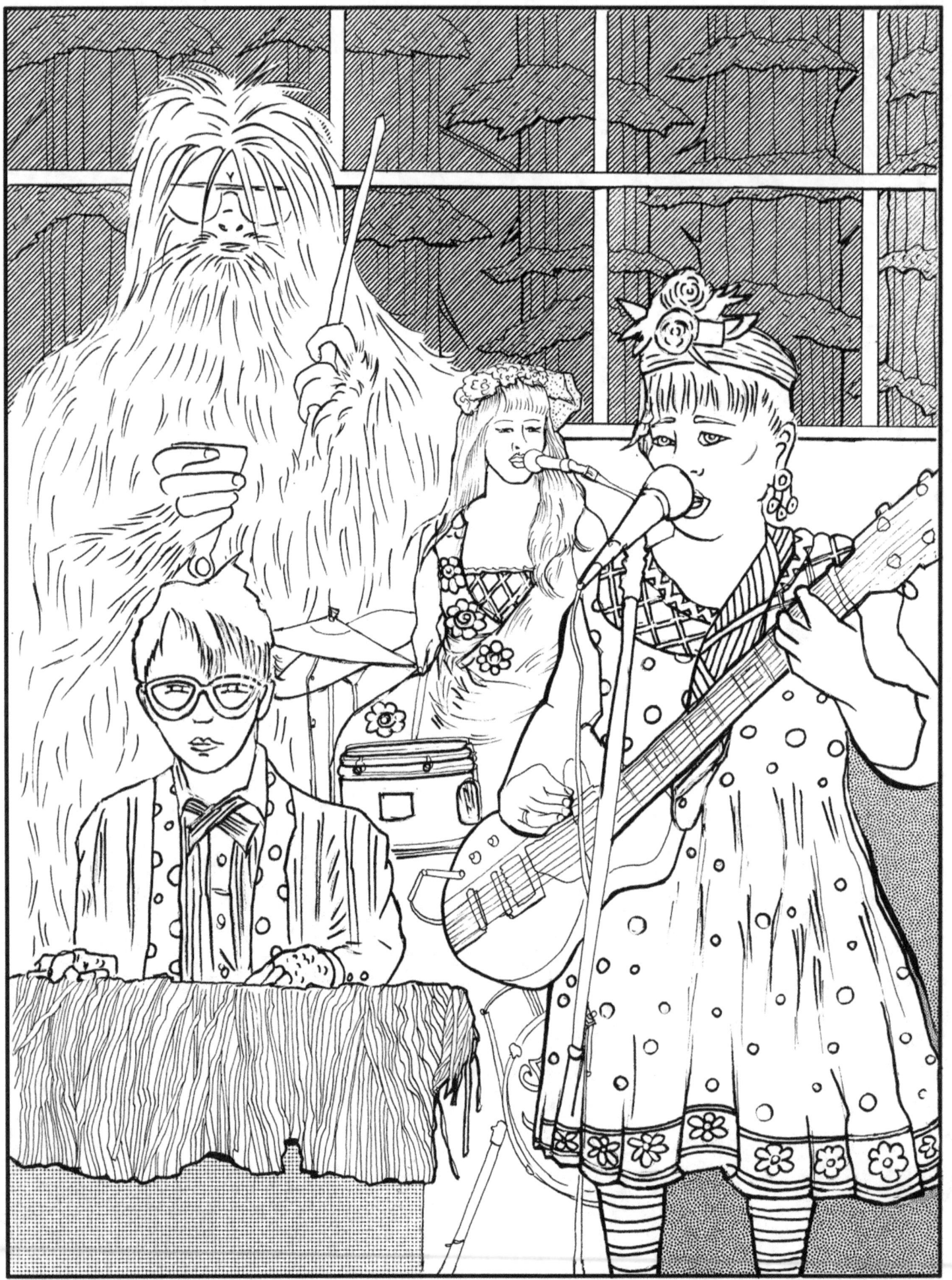

About the Author

K.M. Myers is an illustrator and author, known locally for her involvement in the arts community through art shows, art classes and art pranks most notably the fictitious alt band 50% Amy. She's been a writer for her local publications the *Times Standard* and the *North Coast Journal* as well as lesser known publications such as *Panache Magazine* & *The Dadaist As Liberator*. After completing her Masters of Fine Art in Illustration, she began using the Amazon platform to self-publish her musings.

Other books include:
Drawing Humboldt Step-by-Step Practice Book
Meowasterpieces: A Hisstory of Cat Art

She currently resides in Goudi'ni,
the original name for what is more
commonly known as Arcata, California.

www.ingramcontent.com/pod-product-compliance
Lightning Source LLC
Chambersburg PA
CBHW081018170526
45158CB00010B/3089